# HOME
# COOKING

KING '74

# HOME COOKING

poems by
**Harry Lewis**

photographs by
**Basil King**

MULCH PRESS

*a haystack book*

Mulch Press would like to acknowledge the assistance of The
National Endowment for the Arts and The Coordinating Council
of Literary Magazines which helped make the publication of this
book possible.



**Mulch Press**
**P.O. Box 598**
**Northampton, Mass. 01060**

*New York Office:*
326A Fourth St.
Brooklyn, N. Y. 11215

# CONTENTS

**PHOTOGRAPHS BY BASIL KING**
*pp. 2, 8, 12, 20, 26, 29, 32, 48, 54, 67*

this book is for


David Glotzer
and
Basil King.

                they are both
with me in these poems.




for David
          let me say
that he helped find
this book.

*What I thought was love*
*in me, I find a thousand instances*
*as fear.*

LeRoi Jones


*Love's*
          *no garden in Paradise*
*love*
      *tells us*
             *humming*
*that the stalled motor of*
                    *the heart*
*has started to work*
                *again.*

Vladimir Mayakovsky

# BY AFTERNOON I WAS MOONSTRUCK

all night
the clouds
are fast across
the moon

the path
back to
the house
bright
3/4 full
the wine
3/4 down
my friends
drunk
that
wine-moon

and in the morning
the moon was not that bright
but held the sky
11 a.m. still 3/4
opposite the sun
confused
but floating.

# THE DAILY GRIND
*for David Glotzer*

today
in the mass
of my daily worries
the grind and fears
leaned back on
my cross and tried
to give up my ghost
that bitch that keeps
dogging me and as I
hung there I offered
my body and my
blood to the faithful
but I was not
among them having lost
faith in myself
I was broke
and could not find
a woman (9 months
now) and have fallen
daily into despair
and self-pity
self-disgust
grinds on and on in
my confessions: at
about 4:30
I took some amphetamine
and sang out
in joy like a kiss
of peace *Ite, missa est*
and into whose hands
do I commend
my spirit?

# A ONEWAY TICKET

the young Hindu wants to buy
a oneway ticket
               by bus
from Amherst, Mass. to
Madras, India and
it's 9 a.m. — he's hostile
wants to get home
broke but wants
to go home — oneway.
there's nothing to return to
here — he's wearing sneakers
a light wool
               blue shirt. it's 12 degrees
this morning — how is it with Madras ? he demands
passage. the very proper ticket seller
tells him: you can't get there by bus. she's cornered
and directs him to
the travel bureau in the rear. he insists
he wants to get to Madras: I'll pay you later.
I want to go home.

## AGAIN? AGAIN

*(for B. and D.*
*who found this poem)*


       this City
is no City Of Light
but what I make and in
the last year I've lost
my sense of play and don't
smile but laugh
nervous at the wrong things
like tenderness.

# THE MUSIC
### *for Savuka's Band*


work of joy
(shades)
         ghosts come scat singing
so much more than Orpheus
                     scat
scat SCAT singing the flowers of
my happy day
6 a.m. through
night collecting music (clap hands
clap hands goodtime Harry
wild whistle
            beat tables
hands — clap (hold)
joy-scat (time - time) never such music.
don't look back.

## JAZZ RIFF

I Didn't Know About


about you the piano melts
to sax drum
brushes steady
rhythm
          didn't didn't didn't didn't
I was on top of it all
wandered about
              man about town
but
but
all these things
about town, but
I didn't know about you

not all the words to the song
but the music strong melody
how could?
how could I know about
know about
        about love when
I didn't know
about you? and Monk
on that song
so much I still don't know
about you (?)
          about me

except the melody plays
its way
about love love
how could I know about love
I didn't know about
you? I didn't know about me.
the key is
the solo.

## THE LAST STAND/ SUNDAY MORNING

*for Cathy Standish*


Sunday morning there's
a tender grace hung over the street
I glimpse the story as you walk by
there's nothing on your life
but
a large
        gold ring and
                    a new husband
pulled down the street
dazed in the rush
such
      but for
                the grace of
my tenderness
                go I and
I find Old Standish
out in the cold
                outside the Russian Baths
on East 10th Street. no idea
of
the comfort he could take in
the heat
            210
                to 220
the shock of cold water
to make the skin young

the old men
            so tender
each other
          grace
                they stretch
rubbing down
              such love
there is this gentle truth
there is heaven in such mornings
and I am married to these old men.

## JAZZ RIFF/ Take 1

I Can't Get Started


I've been around my head
to explain
         settled
            nothing
simple or plain
my mind I have charted
still I can't get started
now . . .

## SIRVENTES OF NO PEACE BETWEEN BROTHERS

for Michael

brother
I'd find a weapon
that would break us
against your logic and
my fear

there's no Fall this year
we live our lives
filled around us
you
    your wife
           your son
a daughter
you've gotten fat
gladly
something you've
always wanted

me
can't ever lose enough weight
can't stand how much I eat
and when I visit you
I set limits — the happier
the visit
the less I eat. I tell you
there's this theological argument
between us:

you ask
      logic
and I tell you
I have nothing but faith
that life's between us

and life goes
                even if
                        we don't
I can't stand promises
or cold logic
— a cold meal.

you eat well
to heal the thin body
the meal simmers
we want the same
but I'd be thin
at table
my need no different
is love. your logic

leads to
a family
grows
        and I'm
cut off
with stupid loves
                    I grow
fat on deadends
I still don't see
the proof to your logic
I tell you

if that's my trap
there's no logic
I'd use but eat this Universe
and make it mine
love's no more than love
the future's here
no more than what we do with it
the difference how we take our weight.

## HIDDEN LANGUAGE


in those streets
everything moves.
the heat moves.
the color of houses
rubs off
on my fingers.
rain soaks
the wide avenues of Merida

the Maya
visit
        or work
they hardly talk in this City

                        but there's
a road out through jungles goes
past Chichen: they used to throw children
down the well of Chichen. their bones are still
on the bottom
                and rock. from the road
you can see The House of Dark Writing.
I asked the ticket-taker
                        directions.
on the road south
everything passes
like young pigs
pulled down streets
caught by their back legs
squeal
        death on that rope
and food. the zopolotes

dive
for anything
they think is meat
and in my eyes
that distance is dark
— so much
          I thought
between each creature here
but all that's common is
the marks of living
                    on us.

**GIVING HOURS/ Merida**

they make an art of feeding birds.
clean each feeding station.
give each bird
fresh water
bread and fruit (make
the rounds)

the cripples in uniforms
shine shoes
              under the feeding stations
surrounded by bird-shit
layers of polish
brushed to a smooth finish
10 minutes or more
this is the traffic
the marketplace
the first details of
long mornings. we sit
in the shade of
how many centuries?

to talk
even that takes hours.
days. those old trees
how little we know of
their shade.

**JAZZ RIFF/ Take 2**


I Can't Get Started with


can't get to love. it's
around the world. can't get
no place without proof I am
desired and the broken heart
a warmth makes a revolution
I can't think of myself
                              warmth
makes the bonds more real
OH BUNNY
let me get started. I want
a place with warm arms
slow thrust. some soft thighs

a place with warm arms
shades of mellow
                    that
sweet Bunny Berigan melody
for a life style and somehow
get started.

**SPRING ALCHEMY**


not enough
to be amazed with Spring
                        surprised
                        at the change
but more than that
I feel it in the bones of
an old lady
            dazed
she can't figure out
where she is
                but
the light opens her eyes
her breasts feel alive again
her white hair
turns brown and birds
are flying inside her head. you can see them
through
            her wide eyes
and hear them
when she opens
her mouth
to sing.

**JAZZ RIFF**
     *for Michael Stephens*


Try A Little


get weary
        but try
try
  a little
      tender
        ness
          (advice from
         a friend:
            be tender
try
  don't
     be scarey
     don't be
       hard
try a little. . .
if she is wearing
that same shabby life
stare her in the face.
        it ain't
          sentimental
            but
when she gets weary
when you get weary
try
  try
    the tender
      touch
try/ try

TRY
      a little
tender her
that
      talk softly
but carry
          a big
                heart. . .
the nearness
              of hearts is
tender
        SO — she
may get
and you
may get
        weary
              but come
              and come again
time and
time
again
      try
          just a little
          try
              a little
tender
ness.

## CLOSE TO CALLING IT QUITS WITH SONG




each
those women
one's so young (I kiss her on
her cheek
            tell her
                    call me
one tells me she's
a lesbian (I love her

and the other's
there when I turn
                    waiting to have coffee
and I'm guilty when I tell her
I have nothing to say. she turns.
I don't have time to explain
how much I'd like to need her
                            Love beats me
                            with sticks
                            I cut myself
                            oh
how I'd love them all
believe
        as truth
                everything I wanted
and I'm
the best man
            in the world
and
    the beloved of all
these ladies.

# JAZZ RIFF

Softly As In


a morning sunrise
sun
sun
that heater you have on even in the damp
as we make love I am hotter than
softly as who you are long melodic line
casual
drumbeat
morning
sofffft
ly
assssss in a morning sunnnnn riiiiizzz
as in a morning
I move out one lover's door
and past another lover's door
and up the stairs as through
melodic line I rise
I rise
softly.

**WILL YOU BE MY VALENTINE**

*for K.*


for Valentine's Day
I walk into a room
and all my images
sit at a table:

at the head of the table is
Harry The Poet
and from there
Honest Harry
Rational Harry
Petulant Harry
Shy
Good Humored
Gentle Harry
Dark Harry brooding
Silent Harry and more

the table is shaped like a huge
heart. it is red.
it beats.

you enter and we are
alone. all of us.

**LOOKING FOR LUCK**


up Second Avenue
                really mad
                crazy
                        I pass a penny
surrounded by orange peels
it was its dull copper
                        stood out
I'd gone
            5
                maybe 10 paces when
I decided
I needed the luck

when
        I went back
it was gone
and I'm left
counting myself like
a four-leaf-clover

PAINTS

**SPRING AND**


Spring and
a little lovin'
makes every woman
a charm. I walk in the street
turned on watchin'
everything that has
a female touch (even
the awkward grace of
transvestites.

## DEAR PLANTS


I should love
much more than myself
and
all these notes
                scattered
on my kitchen table

I get up
and paste D E A T H
across the kitchen window
to catch the sun tomorrow
and then
I tell my plants
it does not apply
to them.

**PULSAR**
        *a celebration for a gray day*


I can't control the weather.
                        a gray window
a gray door.
          I have sunspots.
I am rained on. if everything falls
through
there's still the future
to worry about. a star

pulsing in
The Crab Nebula
doesn't give anything
but
thousandths of
seconds — exact
neutron
          pulse (here
feel my heart
              twinkle
little star
          absolute zero — not tense
but dense
enough to
tunnel in on
myself that
          that equilibrium
might again
be possible:

my straw hat
is soaked
            into my hair
drips
down my ears. . . what clock you gonna use

to tell time besides
your own? the pulsars

lose a few seconds
every million years
while I lose
entire days
            caught with
tomorrow and
tomorrow.

# JAZZ RIFF

There Will Never Be


another you
will never be
will never be
be another
you and I can't even
listen to
the radio.
        there will never be
another
another
never be
an
  other
      you
this March comes in
unclear will never be
a lamb will never be
a lion it is
a month will never be
another
be you
then for the last time this morning
I catch the mirror and
sing: there will never be
another
me.

## JAZZ RIFF

Breakfast In Vermont


eggs
and bacon
on a plate
a glass of milk
a cup of tea
                (breakfast in
                    Vermont. . .

morning Autumn chill
dogs barking
                    at
                        the cars
gray
        (slow light
        in
            Vermont

telephone wires
come
down this
landscape
                    traveling
each bend
of my eye

here
caught
in such
romantic setting
and so
hypnotized
                by

wind moving
in the trees
dogs stretching
after sun
            (chilled light
            in
            Vermont.

## HOTDOG

deny all evidence.
go on with life: mustard stains
on my raincoat
right over my heart
are enough
           some days
to bring me to
tears. at those times

I force myself
to remember
the hotdog
and smile.

## ACROSS THE WIDE STORM WHICH IS RAGING

*for Calo Scott*


the storm blows
and I take my apprenticeship
ferrying jazz musicians home in
the worst now
this year: the joy
in crossing
the blind storm
and the melodies
rage
all around
all around

**THE TOWN**


the town of Ware
where? pronounced "wair"
                              what?
                                  where?
who's going where? do you want a ride to
where?
          Ware. listen don't get smart. . .
to where? where is this
Ware? That's where vaudeville got stuck.
the stage: Who stole What
and went Ware..... ?
into the wilderness where we
live. there
in the distance.

# DEAR JANE, GIVE UP THAT CHILD

*for Jane Teller*


sad voice of a woman (old friend
old lover and still new friend
                        sad phone call from
                        New York

                        nothing she says is
specific but the loneliness.

the dogs sleeping downstairs and the dark country
outside:
           in New York, Jane is
awake drunk
and crying. won't
give up her child
in her all these years
crying. dear Jane
give up that child. I know you
as a woman. don't be surprised. I don't
love that child. don't love the child in me
all these years crying to sooth myself
to be a man. I am the man in me
loves you/ can take your call
loves Paul loves David loves Joan
loves Marc loves Basil loves
Martha loves
             Hetty and Mallory who are
children but does not love
the child that is not born
but bears down against
your life and mine and wants
everything. so much better
to grow up
and be kind.

**THE EYE**

it snowed last night.
driving home I kept
into the interior of
the storm. it covered me
and I was
new country
inside this storm
figuring on all
the changes: I was not
Brooklyn. I was
not Second Avenue. I was not
married or drunk
in New York bars. I was
not counting on anything.
I was not past I was
this landscape this season
I was in it
I was not the storm
but watched it
soak into
the ground

## SHIVER YOUR HANDS IN DANCE

*to risa. 3:30 a.m. in my hospital room*

they clean
everything down
here. there is
no sign of
the man who shared
the bed
next to me
        no sign of
the man who died
across the hall. the beds
are made
tight
    everything is
neat
and
finished.

## SIRVENTES IN HOPE OF SONG

*for Paul Blackburn*


I'd turn to give you years
but I can't sing that clear.
distance hung on me
                stalled
                    jammed
had not predicted it was
this bad with you. I find
myself hurt. the catch
is not death is
love.

the breeze stinks. I tell you
I have no taste for the sickness
this Summer holds. I have nothing
that enters bone deep enough
or tenders you
              or speaks clearly enough.
I have never been good at giving myself to anyone.
I wanted to tell you it'll be over soon.
the cancer has moved
             as you say
"to weird places."

what's the reason?
and you tell me over
             again
"to make music"
             and who would break this
'cept death?
        when we can't sing
it comes to a dead-end.

I want to shout at you:
give up that fuckin' innocence.
I never loved that once I learned to love you.
that was not your grace.
I wanted you
to tell those who danced
around you to "fuck off"
the bad music
                    tin ears
drinking "brandy-alexanders in
their polite aunts' drawingrooms.
reading verse. it's not poetry.
they cannot sing."

Keep on about life. it's life
that makes poetry. we'll know your death
only that it's not song. I could not
sing to take you back. I love you now
even if we have not spoken as
I wanted to.

## CANSO
### *for Joan*


she holds me as I kiss her.
just as I get off at my station
I'm sure she wants me but
lets go and it is
my stop. you stop me lady.

# THE NIGHT IN THE BEGGARS TOES

for Mimi

first there is the beggar
with the foot with no toes
he mumbles.

       (it is not that cold yet.
        I've put you in a cab.
the evening is not what I wanted.
but the beggar's night
goes on. he will sit there.
if you saw those toes
           they'd tell you nothing.
they are severed.
the round foot glows under street-lights.
it's me that counts
         the beggar's toes. I
demand alms. I cannot tell you
how much I wanted to hold you
so tight we would both
feel it in our toes. and
then
there are
the couples (as I walked
home) the way they walk
the women leaning into
the men. but
it is
a beggar's night. he holds
the moon in his lost toes.

# THE RUSSIAN LESSON

drunk again
and studying Russian
                    but not on bogka
on bourbon
and I keep pronouncing
the words
          with a southern accent (Georgian ?
yes
    I should've ordered
bogka yaw'all.

**FULL WEAVE**


the spider beside
              the air beside
              my ear
weaves webs of me.

let us hang
            dear friend
mid-air
         delicate.
take the part that's my heart:
                              take my lips.
                              take my arms. weave
through my eyes the network of invisible song. weave
creature
           the song that holds us to
           this world (any world

           we risk all on
           these threads we glide on
           creature,
                    all we have
           is enough to cover
           the distance. hang,
           friend spider
                          by my ear
and sing into me
                  what it is
to climb.

**LOOKING FOR A HOME IN THE COUNTRY**


just follow directions:
North Pleasant Street into what
becomes 63 toward
North Amherst to a sign
off 63 toward 47
                          left
toward Montague Center
                              left
through Center to where
the road divides around
a 2-story red
brick house
                short left
into a huge hill (take it in
second about a mile
past a cemetery covered with ice
'till an arrow points into
a long curve
                  to the right
to the first house
on the right
                white
                      with wire fence
across from the red barn (the frozen graveyard
back down the road
throws me

                the picture of
                ghosts ice-skating
between graves
                    ice cold
lighter than air — such grace
full of the season. . . the edge of
the wind. who knows what wonder lurks

that cold shade knows
what hangs the day on the country road.

## PSALM

down in the valley
(the valley
       so low. . .
it's Spring.
here on this mountain
           (this mountain
               so high
we're
snow-capped.
I woke up with sun in
my eye (here's
sun in your eye and
the first thing I realize
's I've been dreaming
some dark dream
and it's a pleasure to feel
that sweet
       sweet
         light
fall on me and
this mountain ice/ sweet sun
it might as well
be Spring
       when things go
go growing wild.

## THE HARVESTERS


in Bruegel's *The Harvesters*
one of the women stares out
caught eating bread
                    with butter
while the others work
eat soup
          and sleep.
the land
is worked out.
the sea in the distance is
another world. that woman is
bugeyed in the shadow of a tree
as if she saw
Pieter take that picture.

**LETTER**
>*for Marc Shanker*


I am so glad you have confronted the beast of
yourself. that inner lurking that drives us
away from the warmth. I saw it last night
in the shadows of the ice in this New England
Winter. those of us that fall to grief
will pine for love and die: the beast still clawing
to get out.

yesterday it was
a Spring day in January
I was surrounded by women
and warm.
as I sat in the sun breasts circled
around me.
my mouth watered.
Spring goes through us. we
sniff the air/ the heart beats with it.
Marc: we should not
pine for love but set the beast free
to the sun to suck Spring
and thaw the root. it's days like this
when the sap flows
                    I'm no longer afraid
and the heart
does not fall to grief
but opens like
a bud.

**NOTE ON SPRING**


a small dog mounts
a big bitch.
            they lock
and he's frantic
                    as she
walks down
the street.

## JAZZ RIFF

SPRING IS HERE (against the lyric
my heart goes dancing) Spring is here (my heart goes
romancing.
                  even though
                                nobody
                                      loves me
Spring is here
                  on time
this year.

## JAZZ RIFF


The Story Of Love


you've got to give give a little
you've got to give it give
get love
loving. take a little
Spring just for
Spring pushes
                  the story of
just about breaks through
                              the glory of
the world and all its charms
and there are
no roots in love
but love. give a little. . . give give


            the glory is
            a charm.

## HAIR DO (2 VARIATIONS ON A THEME)


*1)*


a young black woman
with her hair done
                    not natural but
like the sculpture on an Italian fountain
                                    twirls
fleur-de-lis. I am expecting the water
to bubble out the top of her head.
she smiles
and we know it's Spring.


*2)*


another view
has her
come to life
in the line and color
Lautrec's posters laughing
doing her hair
                tight and perfect
as her life depended on
ornaments and we
like the artist
                have fallen in love with
her need (the way
she's done it up.

**THE MEAT OF THE TURTLES**

*for n. b.*


her husband draws
women's torsos and
gutted turtles and she's
just had a hysterectomy
the way they put turtles on their backs
on the Isla de Mujeres and cut
their throats in the morning
after she dances with me she tells me
she has evil thoughts she follows
a nervous kid up into a vacant room
the way on the Island of Women
after they cut the beasts' throats
they rip open their bellies. the sea
sudden red. she blows me a kiss as
I leave. it is sadness here
that sickens me. the meat of the turtles
was sweet. the slaughter
whatever it was
was never sad.

# SIRVENTES OF LAST SUMMER'S LOVE

we've begun to talk
                again
and I've caught myself
with
a warm smile
                what would I've done
                if you stayed
                and loved me?

I looked down
saw your shoes
remembered
how I once
started making love to you
as I
removed your shoes.
                naked
                we came
                to Summer
to argue that
                I chased you
and you ran
through all these acts of love

                        Lady
I clear myself toward you.
why should I
smile at what I've already loved?
be warm with cold facts? I am left
to myself to call the worst luck
down on myself. why should
I smile at you
                except
that we both desire
tenderness.

**LOVE POEM**
　　　　for Mary-O


an' now
　　　as aye 'af lurnd

once ya haf left a luv it's
best
　　lef'
　　　　behin'

　　　　　　　an' evin th' roa'
　　　　　　　which once ya hel' tagether
　　　　　　　on a moon night
　　　　　　　　　　　is brokin' now
　　　　　　　　　　　in sof'
　　　　　　　　　　　swee' past/ an'
thar are no pieces 'cept as
the mind flashes now an'
again. . .

## FOR THE JOY OF IT

I will no more of this closing
fear these gray days but
know it is Spring as
the dogs run their games
through the country.

it is warm here
when the sun shines
and the heart is
clear against the trees
the dogs barking for
the joy of it. singing:
this is mine.
the puppy is loudest. *this is
mine.* the mind
and the heart
will no more close on

the season than
the dogs can stop
the birds who know
it is also
theirs.

## A FACT
        *for Mimi*


this is not a love poem
as much as
            a statement of
fact: it is a pleasure
slowly
        and awkwardly
to tell you
            I love you
and let it go
            at that.